Hermit Crabs

Julie Murray

Abdo
FAMILY PETS
Kids

abdopublishing.com

Published by Abdo Kids, a division of ABDO, PO Box 398166, Minneapolis, Minnesota 55439.
Copyright © 2016 by Abdo Consulting Group, Inc. International copyrights reserved in all countries.
No part of this book may be reproduced in any form without written permission from the publisher.

Printed in the United States of America, North Mankato, Minnesota.

052015

092015

 THIS BOOK CONTAINS
RECYCLED MATERIALS

Photo Credits: AP Images, iStock, Landov Media, Shutterstock

Production Contributors: Teddy Borth, Jennie Forsberg, Grace Hansen

Design Contributors: Candice Keimig, Dorothy Toth

Library of Congress Control Number: 2014958425

Cataloging-in-Publication Data

Murray, Julie.

 Hermit crabs / Julie Murray.

  p. cm. -- (Family pets)

ISBN 978-1-62970-903-1

Includes index.

1. Hermit crabs--Juvenile literature. 2. Pets--Juvenile literature.   I. Title.

639'.67--dc23

2014958425

Table of Contents

Hermit Crabs

Hermit crabs make great family pets.

They should not live alone.

Have at least two of them.

They need a **tank**.

It has to be kept clean.

They need sand.

They like to dig.

They need food.

They need **fresh water**.

The also need **salt water**.

They need shells. They change shells as they grow.

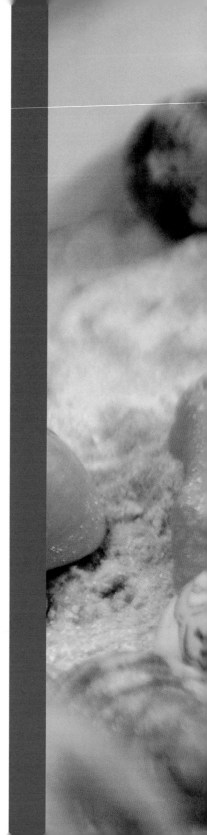

They like to hide. Rocks work well. They like to climb. Sticks will work.

They are fun to watch!

Is a hermit crab the right pet for your family?

Hermit Crab Supplies

driftwood
for climbing

water spray bottle
to keep them wet

extra shells
to grow into

warming bulb
to keep them warm

Glossary

fresh water
water without salt. Most rivers and lakes are fresh water.

salt water
water with salt. Oceans are salt water.

tank
a glass box. A place for small animals to live.

Index

abdokids.com

Use this code to log on to abdokids.com and access crafts, games, videos, and more!

Abdo Kids Code:
FHK9031